BUG OUT

DO-IT-YOURSELF BUG OUT MEALS
FOR DISASTER SURVIVAL

DROPSToNE PRESS
Pocket Field Guide: Bug Out Bag Recipe Book

Copyright © 2020 by Creek Stewart
All Rights Reserved

Author: Jim Ausfahl
Forward by: Creek Stewart
Copyeditor: Jacob Perry

All rights reserved. No part of this book may be reproduced in any form by any
means without express permission of the author. This includes reprints, excerpts,
photocopying, recording or any future means of reproducing text.

If you would like to do any of the above, please seek permission first by
contacting us at http://www.dropstonepress.com

Wholesale inquiries please visit http://www.dropstonepress.com
Purchase this Pocket Field Guide and others in this series at
http://www.creekstewart.com

Published by DROPSToNE PRESS
978-1-947281-24-0

Upon use of any product featured in this manual, you agree to hold harmless Dropstone Press,
LLC and its owners, authors, heirs, employees, including Creek Stewart, of any and all product
liability. You agree that the publisher and abovementioned will not be held responsible or liable for
any direct or indirect loss or injury caused by any product that we publish, produce, promote, and/
or sell. The user assumes full responsibility and all risk related to the use of our products and infor-
mation herein. It is your responsibility to check with local laws regarding legality of items featured
in this manual or any other products that we produce, promote, and/or sell. The items feature in
this manual should not be made or used by anyone under 18 years of age. Any questions about this
liability disclaimer should be directed to contact@dropstonepress.com.

DROPSToNE
—— P R E S S ——
dropstonepress.com

FORWARD

By Creek Stewart

The following text is written by my friend and fellow preparedness enthusiast, Dr. Jim Ausfahl. I met Jim many years ago at an Escape the Woods Survival Training event in Ohio and we've remained friends ever since. He is a humble man; thus, I would like to take a moment to applaud the work he has done here for the preparedness community.

Preparing bulk dry goods into meals can be very overwhelming, especially for single servings. When I first started prepping and storing bulk dry & freeze-dried goods in my home for long-term survival food storage, I can remember struggling with the methods and calculations needed to turn those bags of wheat, beans, rice, oats, and freeze-dried veggies into meals using simple ingredients and preparation methods. I am NOT a "from scratch cook," so formulating meal plans with long term food storage products was a real challenge and one that I've still not totally perfected (2 decades later).

When it comes to long-term food storage, being able to turn those bulk dry & freeze-dried goods into meals is just as important as having them on hand.

As you'll soon see, Jim has created one of the most detailed and meticulously organized meal recipe lists for long-term bulk dry & freeze-dried goods that I've ever seen. He has created these recipes in single-serving sizes, designed as DIY meals for a Bug Out Bag. However, his measurements and instructions can easily be scaled up to meet the needs of families who are preparing bulk dry or freeze-dried ingredients in a BUG IN scenario as well.

This is not only a resource that can be used to prepare meals for Bugging Out but it is a fantastic addition to any well-stocked long-term food storage Bug In pantry as well. Thank you, Jim, for all your hard work on this project! Remember, it's not IF but WHEN,

CR///EK

PREFACE

In a bug out situation, the goal is to get from one place to another, as quickly and safely as possible. Once the route from here to there is known, there are four main issues that a Bug Out Bag (now also known in the military as a Bravo Bag) needs to be able to address: shelter, fire, water, and food (enough for three days as a general rule). Although it is quite possible to go three days without food and still be functional—up to three *weeks* is feasible—it is hardly pleasant. Hence, a small, light stash of food in the Bug Out Bag is reasonable, even if not essential.

In considering what food to store in the Bug Out Bag, knowing that whatever the bag contains is weight that needs carried and space taken up in the bag, items that are light, small and nourishing are preferable. Ideally, since the bag will hopefully sit unused for long periods of time, the material stored should not only be light weight, compact, and high in calories but also have a long shelf life.

It is safe to assume that, in a Bug Out situation, there will be a fire at the start of the day and at the end of the day. Cooking the meals you'll find detailed in these pages can be done over the fire, while you strike camp in the morning or at the end of the day, before retiring. Overall, anything eaten between those two times should be something ready to eat out of the package—perhaps a protein bar or a single serving packet of chicken, tuna, or Spam.

The goal of this text is to provide do-it-yourself recipes for making your own vacuum-sealed, single-serving meals for a Bug Out Bag. The recipes here are all constructed to be added to one cup (240 ml) of water and cooked until the water is fully absorbed; they are then ready to consume. Variations in the grains and other ingredients may change the amount of water needed; I have tried to adjust the recipes so that adding more is the likeliest outcome, rather than having too much water at the start. Each recipe will serve one hungry adult or two younger children. Unless any of the components have a shorter end date, these packets should be stable and safe for approximately one year (likely longer).

With the recipes, I have chosen to use either beef or chicken bouillon or powder. The choice was arbitrary, based on my own preferences. Substituting other bouillons, including vegetable bouillon or fish bouillon, will do, too; just use granular, rather than cube, bouillon.

In all the recipes, adding two tablespoons of bits and pieces of nuts, or adding two tablespoons of dried fruit, will not appreciably change the amount of water needed to prepare the dish. Dried apples or pineapple, for instance, with ham flavored TVP or pork jerky will improve the dish. I am sure you will find other combinations you will like.

Note that the recipes here given do not include any spices. This is not an oversight. Each person needs to adjust the spices and herbs added to their own tastes, especially with the recipes using jerky or dried sausages, now known as meat sticks. The amount of spice in the products varies by the brand

and kind used, and the herbs and spices need to be adjusted to reflect that reality.

In preparing these bags, measure carefully into the vacuum sealable bag; once all the ingredients are in place, seal it, then mark it with the date that it will be out date. Use the shortest date on the packages or one year from the date of your sealing it. Even though all the bags are constructed to use the same amount of water, writing the instructions for cooking it on the vacuum sealed bag is still appropriate:

Add to one cup of potable water; bring to a rolling boil then simmer until water is fully absorbed. Addition of a small amount of water may be needed to achieve the desired consistency.

Should you prefer to make these packets into a *soup*, halve the amount of grain used, and increase the amount of bouillon to 1 ½ teaspoons. To prepare, use 1 ½ cups (360 ml) of water and prepare as above, simmering until the grain is fully cooked and tender. Making a *cream soup* would require the same changes, but also would require adding 1 ½ Tbs of corn starch and 3 ½ tbs powdered milk in the packet. Again, 1 ½ cups of water would be needed to prepare it, and unlike the other recipes, this would need stirred continuously until the grain is fully cooked

These recipes were developed using Harmony House dried vegetables and textured vegetable protein products; it is not certain that the outcomes will be the same with other brands.

CONTENTS

AMARANTH

Amaranth	3 ½ tbs
Beefish Bits	2 ½ tbs
Carrots	1 tsp
Celery	1 tsp
Beef Bouillon or Powder	1 tsp

Amaranth	3 ½ tbs
Beefish Bits	2 tbs
Peppers, mixed	1 tbs
Corn	1 tbs
Beef Bouillon or Powder	1 tsp

Amaranth	3 ½ tbs
Beefish Bits	3 tbs
Broccoli	1 ½ tbs
Beef Bouillon or Powder	1 tsp

Amaranth	3 tbs
Beefish Bits	2 ½ tbs
Sweet Peas	1 tbs
Carrots	1 tbs
Beef Bouillon or Powder	1 tsp

Amaranth	3 ½ tbs
Beefish Bits	2 tbs
Green Beans	1 tbs
Butternut Squash	1 tbs
Beef Bouillon or Powder	1 tsp

. . . .

Amaranth	3 ½ tbs
Chickenish Bits	3 tbs
Carrots	1 tbs
Celery	1 tbs
Chicken Bouillon or Powder	1 tsp

. . . .

Amaranth	3 ½ tbs
Chickenish Bits	3 tbs
Peppers, mixed	1 tbs
Corn	1 tbs
Chicken Bouillon or Powder	1 tsp

. . . .

Amaranth	3 tbs
Chickenish bits	3 tbs
Sweet Peas	1 ½ tbs
Carrots	1 ½ tbs
Chicken Bouillon or Powder	1 tsp

Amaranth	3 ½ tbs
Chickenish bits	3 tbs
Broccoli	4 tbs
Chicken Bouillon or Powder	1 tsp

. . . .

Amaranth	3 tbs
Chickenish bits	3 tbs
Green Beans	1 ½ tbs
Butternut Squash	1 tbs
Chicken Bouillon or Powder	1 tsp

. . . .

Amaranth	3 ½ tbs
Hamish Bits	3 tbs
Carrots	1 tbs
Celery	1 tbs
Chicken Bouillon or Powder	1 tsp

. . . .

Amaranth	3 ½ tbs
Hamish Bits	3 tbs
Peppers, mixed	1 tbs
Corn	1 tbs
Chicken Bouillon or Powder	1 tsp

Amaranth	3 ½ tbs
Hamish Bits	3 tbs
Sweet Peas	2 tbs
Chicken Bouillon or Powder	1 tsp

. . . .

Amaranth	3 ½ tbs
Hamish Bits	3 tbs
Green Beans	1 tbs
Butternut Squash	1 tbs
Chicken Bouillon or Powder	1 tsp

. . . .

Amaranth	3 ½ tbs
Hamish Bits	3 ½ tbs
Broccoli	2 ½ tbs
Chicken Bouillon or Powder	1 tsp

. . . .

Amaranth	3 tbs
Hamish Bits	3 ½ tbs
Sweet Peas	1 ½ tbs
Carrots	1 tbs
Chicken Bouillon or Powder	1 tsp

Amaranth	3 ½ tbs
Jerky	2 oz
Green Beans	2 ½ tbs
Butternut Squash	2 tbs
Beef Bouillon or Powder	1 tsp

. . . .

Amaranth	3 ½ tbs
Jerky	2 oz
Green Beans	2 ½ tbs
Butternut Squash	2 tbs
Beef Bouillon or Powder	1 tsp

. . . .

Amaranth	5 tbs
Jerky	2 oz
Broccoli	2 ½ tbs
Beef Bouillon or Powder	1 tsp

. . . .

Amaranth	4 tbs
Jerky	2 oz
Green Beans	2 tbs
Butternut Squash	1 ½ tbs
Beef Bouillon or Powder	1 tsp

Amaranth	4 ½ tbs
Jerky	2 oz
Sweet Peas	1 ½ tbs
Carrots	1 tbs
Beef Bouillon or Powder	1 tsp

....

Amaranth	4 ½ tbs
Jerky	2 oz
Carrots	1 tbs
Celery	1 tbs
Beef Bouillon or Powder	1 tsp

....

Amaranth	4 ½ tbs
Jerky	2 oz
Peppers, mixed	1 ½ tbs
Corn	2 tbs
Beef Bouillon or Powder	1 tsp

BARLEY

Barley	3 tbs
Beefish Bits	4 tbs
Carrots	2 tsp
Celery	2 tsp
Beef Bouillon or Powder	1 tsp

Barley	3 ½ tbs
Beefish Bits	3 tbs
Peppers, mixed	1 tbs
Corn	1 tbs
Beef Bouillon or Powder	1 tsp

Barley	4 tbs
Beefish Bits	3 tbs
Broccoli	2 tbs
Beef Bouillon or Powder	1 tsp

Barley	4 tbs
Beefish Bits	2 tbs
Sweet Peas	1 tbs
Carrots	1 tbs
Beef Bouillon or Powder	1 tsp

Barley	3 ½ tbs
Beefish Bits	2 ½ tbs
Green Beans	1 tbs
Butternut Squash	1 tbs
Beef Bouillon or Powder	1 tsp

....

Barley	3 ½ tbs
Chickenish Bits	4 tbs
Carrots	1 tbs
Celery	1 tbs
Chicken Bouillon or Powder	1 tsp

....

Barley	3 ½ tbs
Chickenish Bits	4 tbs
Peppers, mixed	1 tbs
Corn	1 tbs
Chicken Bouillon or Powder	1 tsp

....

Barley	3 ½ tbs
Chickenish bits	3 tbs
Sweet Peas	1 ½ tbs
Carrots	1 ½ tbs
Chicken Bouillon or Powder	1 tsp

Barley	4 tbs
Chickenish bits	3 ½ tbs
Broccoli	2 ½ tbs
Chicken Bouillon or Powder	1 tsp

. . . .

Barley	3 ½ tbs
Chickenish bits	3 tbs
Green Beans	1 ½ tbs
Butternut Squash	1 tbs
Chicken Bouillon or Powder	1 tsp

. . . .

Barley	4 tbs
Hamish Bits	3 tbs
Carrots	1 tbs
Celery	1 tbs
Chicken Bouillon or Powder	1 tsp

. . . .

Barley	4 tbs
Hamish Bits	3 tbs
Peppers, mixed	1 ½ tbs
Corn	1 tbs
Chicken Bouillon or Powder	1 tsp

Barley	3 ½ tbs
Hamish Bits	4 tbs
Sweet Peas	2 ½ tbs
Chicken Bouillon or Powder	1 tsp

. . . .

Barley	3 tbs
Hamish Bits	3 tbs
Green Beans	2 tbs
Butternut Squash	2 tbs
Chicken Bouillon or Powder	1 tsp

. . . .

Barley	4 tbs
Hamish Bits	3 ½ tbs
Broccoli	3 ½ tbs
Chicken Bouillon or Powder	1 tsp

. . . .

Barley	4 tbs
Hamish Bits	3 ½ tbs
Sweet Peas	1 ½ tbs
Carrots	1 tbs
Chicken Bouillon or Powder	1 tsp

Barley	4 tbs
Jerky	2 oz
Green Beans	3 tbs
Butternut Squash	2 tbs
Beef Bouillon or Powder	1 tsp

. . . .

Barley	5 tbs
Jerky	2 oz
Green Beans	2 tbs
Butternut Squash	1 ½ tbs
Beef Bouillon or Powder	1 tsp

. . . .

Barley	6 tbs
Jerky	2 oz
Broccoli	2 ½ tbs
Beef Bouillon or Powder	1 tsp

. . . .

Barley	5 tbs
Jerky	2 oz
Green Beans	2 tbs
Butternut Squash	1 tbs
Beef Bouillon or Powder	1 tsp

Barley	5 tbs
Jerky	2 oz
Sweet Peas	1 ½ tbs
Carrots	1 ½ tbs
Beef Bouillon or Powder	1 tsp

....

Barley	4 ½ tbs
Jerky	2 oz
Carrots	2 tbs
Celery	2 tbs
Beef Bouillon or Powder	1 tsp

....

Barley	5 ½ tbs
Jerky	2 oz
Peppers, mixed	1 ½ tbs
Corn	2 tbs
Beef Bouillon or Powder	1 tsp

BUCKWHEAT

Buckwheat	4 tbs
Beefish Bits	3 ½ tbs
Carrots	2 tsp
Celery	2 tsp
Beef Bouillon or Powder	1 tsp

Buckwheat	4 tbs
Beefish Bits	3 tbs
Peppers, mixed	1 ½ tbs
Corn	1 ½ tbs
Beef Bouillon or Powder	1 tsp

Buckwheat	4 ½ tbs
Beefish Bits	3 tbs
Broccoli	3 ½ tbs
Beef Bouillon or Powder	1 tsp

Buckwheat	4 ½ tbs
Beefish Bits	2 ½ tbs
Sweet Peas	1 tbs
Carrots	1 tbs
Beef Bouillon or Powder	1 tsp

Buckwheat	4 ½ tbs
Beefish Bits	2 ½ tbs
Green Beans	1 tbs
Butternut Squash	1 tbs
Beef Bouillon or Powder	1 tsp

....

Buckwheat	4 tbs
Chickenish Bits	4 tbs
Carrots	1 tbs
Celery	1 ½ tbs
Chicken Bouillon or Powder	1 tsp

....

Buckwheat	4 tbs
Chickenish Bits	4 tbs
Peppers, mixed	1 ½ tbs
Corn	1 tbs
Chicken Bouillon or Powder	1 tsp

....

Buckwheat	4 tbs
Chickenish bits	4 tbs
Sweet Peas	1 ½ tbs
Carrots	1 tbs
Chicken Bouillon or Powder	1 tsp

Buckwheat	4 ½ tbs
Chickenish bits	4 tbs
Broccoli	3 tbs
Chicken Bouillon or Powder	1 tsp

. . . .

Buckwheat	4 tbs
Chickenish bits	3 tbs
Green Beans	1 ½ tbs
Butternut Squash	1 ½ tbs
Chicken Bouillon or Powder	1 tsp

. . . .

Buckwheat	4 ½ tbs
Hamish Bits	4 tbs
Carrots	1 tbs
Celery	1 tbs
Chicken Bouillon or Powder	1 tsp

. . . .

Buckwheat	4 ½ tbs
Hamish Bits	4 tbs
Peppers, mixed	1 ½ tbs
Corn	1 tbs
Chicken Bouillon or Powder	1 tsp

Buckwheat	4 tbs
Hamish Bits	4 tbs
Sweet Peas	3 tbs
Chicken Bouillon or Powder	1 tsp

. . . .

Buckwheat	4 tbs
Jerky	2 oz
Green Beans	3 tbs
Butternut Squash	3 tbs
Beef Bouillon or Powder	1 tsp

. . . .

Buckwheat	7 ½ tbs
Jerky	2 oz
Broccoli	2 ½ tbs
Beef Bouillon or Powder	1 tsp

. . . .

Buckwheat	7 tbs
Jerky	2 oz
Green Beans	1 tbs
Butternut Squash	1 tbs
Beef Bouillon or Powder	1 tsp

Buckwheat	7 tbs
Jerky	2 oz
Sweet Peas	1 ½ tbs
Carrots	1 tbs
Beef Bouillon or Powder	1 tsp

. . . .

Buckwheat	7 tbs
Jerky	2 oz
Carrots	1 tbs
Celery	1 tbs
Beef Bouillon or Powder	1 tsp

. . . .

Buckwheat	7 tbs
Jerky	2 oz
Peppers, mixed	1 tbs
Corn	2 tbs
Beef Bouillon or Powder	1 tsp

BULGUR

Bulgur	3 ½ tbs
Beefish Bits	4 tbs
Carrots	2 tsp
Celery	2 tsp
Beef Bouillon or Powder	1 tsp

. . . .

Bulgur	4 tbs
Beefish Bits	3 ½ tbs
Peppers, mixed	1 tbs
Corn	1 tbs
Beef Bouillon or Powder	1 tsp

. . . .

Bulgur	4 tbs
Beefish Bits	3 ½ tbs
Broccoli	3 tbs
Beef Bouillon or Powder	1 tsp

. . . .

Bulgur	4 ½ tbs
Beefish Bits	2 ½ tbs
Sweet Peas	1 tbs
Carrots	1 tbs
Beef Bouillon or Powder	1 tsp

Bulgur	4 ½ tbs
Beefish Bits	2 tbs
Green Beans	1 ½ tbs
Butternut Squash	1 ½ tbs
Beef Bouillon or Powder	1 tsp

. . . .

Bulgur	4 ½ tbs
Chickenish Bits	4 tbs
Carrots	1 tbs
Celery	1 tbs
Chicken Bouillon or Powder	1 tsp

. . . .

Bulgur	4 ½ tbs
Chickenish Bits	3 tbs
Peppers, mixed	2 tbs
Corn	1 ½ tbs
Chicken Bouillon or Powder	1 tsp

. . . .

Bulgur	4 tbs
Chickenish bits	4 tbs
Sweet Peas	1 ½ tbs
Carrots	1 tbs
Chicken Bouillon or Powder	1 tsp

Bulgur	4 ½ tbs
Chickenish bits	4 ½ tbs
Broccoli	2 tbs
Chicken Bouillon or Powder	1 tsp

. . . .

Bulgur	4 tbs
Chickenish bits	4 tbs
Green Beans	1 tbs
Butternut Squash	1 ½ tbs
Chicken Bouillon or Powder	1 tsp

. . . .

Bulgur	4 tbs
Hamish Bits	4 ½ tbs
Carrots	1 tbs
Celery	1 tbs
Chicken Bouillon or Powder	1 tsp

. . . .

Bulgur	4 tbs
Hamish Bits	4 ½ tbs
Peppers, mixed	1 ½ tbs
Corn	1 tbs
Chicken Bouillon or Powder	1 tsp

Bulgur	4 tbs
Hamish Bits	5 tbs
Sweet Peas	2 ½ tbs
Chicken Bouillon or Powder	1 tsp

....

Bulgur	3 ½ tbs
Hamish Bits	4 tbs
Green Beans	1 ½ tbs
Butternut Squash	1 ½ tbs
Chicken Bouillon or Powder	1 tsp

....

Bulgur	5 tbs
Hamish Bits	4 tbs
Broccoli	2 tbs
Chicken Bouillon or Powder	1 tsp

....

Bulgur	4 ½ tbs
Hamish Bits	3 ½ tbs
Sweet Peas	1 ½ tbs
Carrots	1 tbs
Chicken Bouillon or Powder	1 tsp

Bulgur	4 ½ tbs
Jerky	2 oz
Green Beans	3 tbs
Butternut Squash	2 ½ tbs
Beef Bouillon or Powder	1 tsp

. . . .

Bulgur	4 ½ tbs
Jerky	2 oz
Green Beans	3 tbs
Butternut Squash	3 tbs
Beef Bouillon or Powder	1 tsp

. . . .

Bulgur	7 ½ tbs
Jerky	2 oz
Broccoli	2 ½ tbs
Beef Bouillon or Powder	1 tsp

. . . .

Bulgur	7 tbs
Jerky	2 oz
Green Beans	1 tbs
Butternut Squash	1 tbs
Beef Bouillon or Powder	1 tsp

Bulgur	7 tbs
Jerky	2 oz
Sweet Peas	1 tbs
Carrots	1 tbs
Beef Bouillon or Powder	1 tsp

....

Bulgur	7 tbs
Jerky	2 oz
Carrots	1 tbs
Celery	1 tbs
Beef Bouillon or Powder	1 tsp

....

Bulgur	7 tbs
Jerky	2 oz
Peppers, mixed	1 tbs
Corn	2 tbs
Beef Bouillon or Powder	1 tsp

CRACKED WHEAT

Cracked Wheat	3 tbs
Beefish Bits	3 tbs
Carrots	2 tsp
Celery	2 tsp
Beef Bouillon or Powder	1 tsp

Cracked Wheat	3 tbs
Beefish Bits	3 tbs
Peppers, mixed	1 tbs
Corn	1 tbs
Beef Bouillon or Powder	1 tsp

Cracked Wheat	3 tbs
Beefish Bits	3 tbs
Broccoli	3 tbs
Beef Bouillon or Powder	1 tsp

Cracked Wheat	3 tbs
Beefish Bits	2 ½ tbs
Sweet Peas	1 tbs
Carrots	1 tbs
Beef Bouillon or Powder	1 tsp

Cracked Wheat	3 ½ tbs
Beefish Bits	2 tbs
Green Beans	1 tbs
Butternut Squash	1 tbs
Beef Bouillon or Powder	1 tsp

. . . .

Cracked Wheat	3 tbs
Chickenish Bits	3 tbs
Carrots	1 ½ tbs
Celery	1 tbs
Chicken Bouillon or Powder	1 tsp

. . . .

Cracked Wheat	3 ½ tbs
Chickenish Bits	3 tbs
Peppers, mixed	1 tbs
Corn	1 tbs
Chicken Bouillon or Powder	1 tsp

. . . .

Cracked Wheat	3 tbs
Chickenish bits	3 tbs
Sweet Peas	1 ½ tbs
Carrots	1 ½ tbs
Chicken Bouillon or Powder	1 tsp

Cracked Wheat	3 ½ tbs
Chickenish bits	3 tbs
Broccoli	3 tbs
Chicken Bouillon or Powder	1 tsp

. . . .

Cracked Wheat	3 tbs
Chickenish bits	3 tbs
Green Beans	1 ½ tbs
Butternut Squash	1 tbs
Chicken Bouillon or Powder	1 tsp

. . . .

Cracked Wheat	3 ½ tbs
Hamish Bits	3 tbs
Carrots	1 tbs
Celery	1 tbs
Chicken Bouillon or Powder	1 tsp

. . . .

Cracked Wheat	3 ½ tbs
Hamish Bits	3 tbs
Peppers, mixed	1 tbs
Corn	1 tbs
Chicken Bouillon or Powder	1 tsp

Cracked Wheat	3 ½ tbs
Hamish Bits	3 tbs
Sweet Peas	2 tbs
Chicken Bouillon or Powder	1 tsp

. . . .

Cracked Wheat	3 ½ tbs
Hamish Bits	3 tbs
Green Beans	1 tbs
Butternut Squash	1 tbs
Chicken Bouillon or Powder	1 tsp

. . . .

Cracked Wheat	3 ½ tbs
Hamish Bits	3 ½ tbs
Broccoli	2 ½ tbs
Chicken Bouillon or Powder	1 tsp

. . . .

Cracked Wheat	3 tbs
Hamish Bits	3 ½ tbs
Sweet Peas	1 ½ tbs
Carrots	1 tbs
Chicken Bouillon or Powder	1 tsp

Cracked Wheat	3 tbs
Jerky	2 oz
Green Beans	3 tbs
Butternut Squash	2 ½ tbs
Beef Bouillon or Powder	1 tsp

. . . .

Cracked Wheat	4 tbs
Jerky	2 oz
Green Beans	1 ½ tbs
Butternut Squash	1 ½ tbs
Beef Bouillon or Powder	1 tsp

. . . .

Cracked Wheat	5 tbs
Jerky	2 oz
Broccoli	2 ½ tbs
Beef Bouillon or Powder	1 tsp

. . . .

Cracked Wheat	4 tbs
Jerky	2 oz
Green Beans	2 tbs
Butternut Squash	1 ½ tbs
Beef Bouillon or Powder	1 tsp

Cracked Wheat	4 ½ tbs
Jerky	2 oz
Sweet Peas	1 ½ tbs
Carrots	1 tbs
Beef Bouillon or Powder	1 tsp

- -

Cracked Wheat	4 ½ tbs
Jerky	2 oz
Carrots	1 tbs
Celery	1 tbs
Beef Bouillon or Powder	1 tsp

- -

Cracked Wheat	4 ½ tbs
Jerky	2 oz
Peppers, mixed	1 ½ tbs
Corn	2 tbs
Beef Bouillon or Powder	1 tsp

COOKED, DRIED GARBANZOS

Cooked, Dried Garbanzos	5 tbs
Beefish Bits	4 tbs
Carrots	2 tsp
Celery	2 tsp
Beef Bouillon or Powder	1 tsp

. . . .

Cooked, Dried Garbanzos	6 tbs
Beefish Bits	3 tbs
Peppers, mixed	1 tbs
Corn	2 tbs
Beef Bouillon or Powder	1 tsp

. . . .

Cooked, Dried Garbanzos	6 tbs
Beefish Bits	3 ½ tbs
Broccoli	2 ½ tbs
Beef Bouillon or Powder	1 tsp

. . . .

Cooked, Dried Garbanzos	5 tbs
Beefish Bits	3 tbs
Sweet Peas	1 ½ tbs
Carrots	1 ½ tbs
Beef Bouillon or Powder	1 tsp

Cooked, Dried Garbanzos	5 tbs
Beefish Bits	3 tbs
Green Beans	1 ½ tbs
Butternut Squash	1 ½ tbs
Beef Bouillon or Powder	1 tsp

....

Cooked, Dried Garbanzos	5 tbs
Chickenish Bits	4 tbs
Carrots	1 ½ tbs
Celery	1 ½ tbs
Chicken Bouillon or Powder	1 tsp

....

Cooked, Dried Garbanzos	5 tbs
Chickenish Bits	4 tbs
Peppers, mixed	2 tbs
Corn	1 ½ tbs
Chicken Bouillon or Powder	1 tsp

....

Cooked, Dried Garbanzos	5 tbs
Chickenish bits	4 ½ tbs
Sweet Peas	1 ½ tbs
Carrots	1 tbs
Chicken Bouillon or Powder	1 tsp

Cooked, Dried Garbanzos	6 tbs
Chickenish bits	4 ½ tbs
Broccoli	3 tbs
Chicken Bouillon or Powder	1 tsp

. . . .

Cooked, Dried Garbanzos	5 tbs
Chickenish bits	4 ½ tbs
Green Beans	1 tbs
Butternut Squash	1 tbs
Chicken Bouillon or Powder	1 tsp

. . . .

Cooked, Dried Garbanzos	5 tbs
Hamish Bits	4 ½ tbs
Carrots	1 ½ tbs
Celery	1 ½ tbs
Chicken Bouillon or Powder	1 tsp

. . . .

Cooked, Dried Garbanzos	5 tbs
Hamish Bits	4 ½ tbs
Peppers, mixed	2 tbs
Corn	1 ½ tbs
Chicken Bouillon or Powder	1 tsp

Cooked, Dried Garbanzos	5 ½ tbs
Hamish Bits	5 tbs
Sweet Peas	2 tbs
Chicken Bouillon or Powder	1 tsp

. . . .

Cooked, Dried Garbanzos	5 tbs
Hamish Bits	5 tbs
Green Beans	1 ½ tbs
Butternut Squash	1 tbs
Chicken Bouillon or Powder	1 tsp

. . . .

Cooked, Dried Garbanzos	6 tbs
Hamish Bits	5 tbs
Broccoli	3 tbs
Chicken Bouillon or Powder	1 tsp

. . . .

Cooked, Dried Garbanzos	6 tbs
Hamish Bits	3 ½ tbs
Sweet Peas	1 ½ tbs
Carrots	1 tbs
Chicken Bouillon or Powder	1 tsp

Cooked, Dried Garbanzos	6 tbs
Jerky	2 oz
Green Beans	3 tbs
Butternut Squash	3 tbs
Beef Bouillon or Powder	1 tsp

. . . .

Cooked, Dried Garbanzos	7 tbs
Jerky	2 oz
Green Beans	2 tbs
Butternut Squash	2 ½ tbs
Beef Bouillon or Powder	1 tsp

. . . .

Cooked, Dried Garbanzos	10 tbs
Jerky	2 oz
Broccoli	4 tbs
Beef Bouillon or Powder	1 tsp

. . . .

Cooked, Dried Garbanzos	8 tbs
Jerky	2 oz
Green Beans	2 tbs
Butternut Squash	1 ½ tbs
Beef Bouillon or Powder	1 tsp

Cooked, Dried Garbanzos	9 tbs
Jerky	2 oz
Sweet Peas	1 ½ tbs
Carrots	1 tbs
Beef Bouillon or Powder	1 tsp

. . . .

Cooked, Dried Garbanzos	9 ½ tbs
Jerky	2 oz
Carrots	1 tbs
Celery	1 tbs
Beef Bouillon or Powder	1 tsp

. . . .

Cooked, Dried Garbanzos	9 ½ tbs
Jerky	2 oz
Peppers, mixed	1 ½ tbs
Corn	2 tbs
Beef Bouillon or Powder	1 tsp

LENTILS

Lentils	3 tbs
Beefish Bits	3 tbs
Carrots	2 tsp
Celery	2 tsp
Beef Bouillon or Powder	1 tsp

Lentils	3 tbs
Beefish Bits	3 tbs
Peppers, mixed	1 tbs
Corn	1 tbs
Beef Bouillon or Powder	1 tsp

Lentils	4 tbs
Beefish Bits	2 tbs
Broccoli	1 ½ tbs
Beef Bouillon or Powder	1 tsp

Lentils	3 tbs
Beefish Bits	2 ½ tbs
Sweet Peas	1 tbs
Carrots	1 tbs
Beef Bouillon or Powder	1 tsp

Lentils	3 ½ tbs
Beefish Bits	2 tbs
Green Beans	1 tbs
Butternut Squash	1 tbs
Beef Bouillon or Powder	1 tsp

. . . .

Lentils	3 ½ tbs
Chickenish Bits	3 tbs
Peppers, mixed	1 tbs
Corn	1 tbs
Chicken Bouillon or Powder	1 tsp

. . . .

Lentils	3 tbs
Chickenish bits	3 tbs
Sweet Peas	1 ½ tbs
Carrots	1 ½ tbs
Chicken Bouillon or Powder	1 tsp

. . . .

Lentils	3 ½ tbs
Chickenish bits	3 tbs
Broccoli	3 tbs
Chicken Bouillon or Powder	1 tsp

Lentils	3 tbs
Chickenish bits	3 tbs
Green Beans	1 ½ tbs
Butternut Squash	1 tbs
Chicken Bouillon or Powder	1 tsp

. . . .

Lentils	3 ½ tbs
Hamish Bits	3 tbs
Carrots	1 tbs
Celery	1 tbs
Chicken Bouillon or Powder	1 tsp

. . . .

Lentils	3 ½ tbs
Hamish Bits	3 tbs
Peppers, mixed	1 tbs
Corn	1 tbs
Chicken Bouillon or Powder	1 tsp

. . . .

Lentils	3 ½ tbs
Hamish Bits	3 tbs
Sweet Peas	2 tbs
Chicken Bouillon or Powder	1 tsp

Lentils	3 tbs
Hamish Bits	2 ½ tbs
Green Beans	2 tbs
Butternut Squash	1 tbs
Chicken Bouillon or Powder	1 tsp

. . . .

Lentils	4 tbs
Hamish Bits	3 tbs
Broccoli	1 ½ tbs
Chicken Bouillon or Powder	1 tsp

. . . .

Lentils	3 tbs
Hamish Bits	3 ½ tbs
Sweet Peas	1 ½ tbs
Carrots	1 tbs
Chicken Bouillon or Powder	1 tsp

. . . .

Lentils	3 ½ tbs
Jerky	2 oz
Green Beans	2 ½ tbs
Butternut Squash	2 tbs
Beef Bouillon or Powder	1 tsp

Lentils	4 tbs
Jerky	2 oz
Green Beans	1 ½ tbs
Butternut Squash	1 ½ tbs
Beef Bouillon or Powder	1 tsp

. . . .

Lentils	5 tbs
Jerky	2 oz
Broccoli	3 tbs
Beef Bouillon or Powder	1 tsp

. . . .

Lentils	4 tbs
Jerky	2 oz
Green Beans	1 ½ tbs
Butternut Squash	1 ½ tbs
Beef Bouillon or Powder	1 tsp

. . . .

Lentils	4 ½ tbs
Jerky	2 oz
Sweet Peas	1 ½ tbs
Carrots	1 tbs
Beef Bouillon or Powder	1 tsp

Lentils	4 ½ tbs
Jerky	2 oz
Carrots	1 tbs
Celery	1 tbs
Beef Bouillon or Powder	1 tsp

. . . .

Lentils	4 ½ tbs
Jerky	2 oz
Peppers, mixed	1 ½ tbs
Corn	2 tbs
Beef Bouillon or Powder	1 tsp

POTATOES, DICED & DRIED

Potatoes, Diced & Dried	6 ½ tbs
Beefish Bits	4 tbs
Carrots	2 tsp
Celery	2 tsp
Beef Bouillon or Powder	1 tsp

. . . .

Potatoes, Diced & Dried	7 tbs
Beefish Bits	3 tbs
Peppers, mixed	2 tbs
Corn	2 tbs
Beef Bouillon or Powder	1 tsp

. . . .

Potatoes, Diced & Dried	7 ½ tbs
Beefish Bits	3 ½ tbs
Broccoli	4 tbs
Beef Bouillon or Powder	1 tsp

. . . .

Potatoes, Diced & Dried	7 tbs
Beefish Bits	3 tbs
Sweet Peas	1 ½ tbs
Carrots	1 ½ tbs
Beef Bouillon or Powder	1 tsp

Potatoes, Diced & Dried	7 tbs
Beefish Bits	3 tbs
Green Beans	1 ½ tbs
Butternut Squash	1 tbs
Beef Bouillon or Powder	1 tsp

. . . .

Potatoes, Diced & Dried	5 tbs
Chickenish Bits	5 tbs
Carrots	1 ½ tbs
Celery	1 ½ tbs
Chicken Bouillon or Powder	1 tsp

. . . .

Potatoes, Diced & Dried	4 tbs
Chickenish Bits	5 tbs
Peppers, mixed	1 ½ tbs
Corn	1 ½ tbs
Chicken Bouillon or Powder	1 tsp

. . . .

Potatoes, Diced & Dried	6 tbs
Chickenish bits	4 ½ tbs
Sweet Peas	1 ½ tbs
Carrots	1 ½ tbs
Chicken Bouillon or Powder	1 tsp

Potatoes, Diced & Dried	9 tbs
Chickenish bits	4 tbs
Broccoli	7 tsp
Chicken Bouillon or Powder	1 tsp

. . . .

Potatoes, Diced & Dried	7 tbs
Chickenish bits	4 tbs
Green Beans	1 ½ tbs
Butternut Squash	1 tbs
Chicken Bouillon or Powder	1 tsp

. . . .

Potatoes, Diced & Dried	7 tbs
Hamish Bits	4 tbs
Carrots	1 ½ tbs
Celery	1 ½ tbs
Chicken Bouillon or Powder	1 tsp

. . . .

Potatoes, Diced & Dried	7 tbs
Hamish Bits	4 tbs
Peppers, mixed	2 ½ tbs
Corn	2 tbs
Chicken Bouillon or Powder	1 tsp

Potatoes, Diced & Dried	8 tbs
Hamish Bits	4 ½ tbs
Sweet Peas	2 tbs
Chicken Bouillon or Powder	1 tsp

. . . .

Potatoes, Diced & Dried	7 tbs
Hamish Bits	4 tbs
Green Beans	1 ½ tbs
Butternut Squash	1 ½ tbs
Chicken Bouillon or Powder	1 tsp

. . . .

Potatoes, Diced & Dried	7 ½ tbs
Hamish Bits	5 ½ tbs
Broccoli	3 tbs
Beef Bouillon or Powder	1 tsp

. . . .

Potatoes, Diced & Dried	8 tbs
Hamish Bits	3 ½ tbs
Sweet Peas	1 ½ tbs
Carrots	1 tbs
Chicken Bouillon or Powder	1 tsp

Potatoes, Diced & Dried	7 tbs
Jerky	2 oz
Green Beans	3 ½ tbs
Butternut Squash	3 tbs
Beef Bouillon or Powder	1 tsp

....

Potatoes, Diced & Dried	8 tbs
Jerky	2 oz
Green Beans	3 tbs
Butternut Squash	3 tbs
Beef Bouillon or Powder	1 tsp

....

Potatoes, Diced & Dried	13 tbs
Jerky	2 oz
Broccoli	5 tbs
Beef Bouillon or Powder	1 tsp

....

Potatoes, Diced & Dried	9 tbs
Jerky	2 oz
Green Beans	2 ½ tbs
Butternut Squash	2 ½ tbs
Beef Bouillon or Powder	1 tsp

Potatoes, Diced & Dried	10 tbs
Jerky	2 oz
Sweet Peas	2 tbs
Carrots	2 ½ tbs
Beef Bouillon or Powder	1 tsp

....

Potatoes, Diced & Dried	10 tbs
Jerky	2 oz
Carrots	2 ½ tbs
Celery	2 tbs
Beef Bouillon or Powder	1 tsp

....

Potatoes, Diced & Dried	11 tbs
Jerky	2 oz
Peppers, mixed	3 tbs
Corn	2 ½ tbs
Beef Bouillon or Powder	1 tsp

QUINOA

Quinoa	4 tbs
Beefish Bits	3 ½ tbs
Carrots	2 tsp
Celery	2 tsp
Beef Bouillon or Powder	1 tsp

. . . .

Quinoa	4 tbs
Beefish Bits	3 ½ tbs
Peppers, mixed	1 tbs
Corn	1 ½ tbs
Beef Bouillon or Powder	1 tsp

. . . .

Quinoa	5 tbs
Beefish Bits	3 tbs
Broccoli	2 tbs
Beef Bouillon or Powder	1 tsp

. . . .

Quinoa	4 ½ tbs
Beefish Bits	2 ½ tbs
Sweet Peas	1 tbs
Carrots	1 tbs
Beef Bouillon or Powder	1 tsp

Quinoa	4 ½ tbs
Hamish Bits	4 tbs
Sweet Peas	2 tbs
Chicken Bouillon or Powder	1 tsp

. . . .

Quinoa	4 tbs
Hamish Bits	3 ½ tbs
Green Beans	1 ½ tbs
Butternut Squash	1 ½ tbs
Chicken Bouillon or Powder	1 tsp

. . . .

Quinoa	4 ½ tbs
Hamish Bits	4 tbs
Broccoli	2 tbs
Chicken Bouillon or Powder	1 tsp

. . . .

Quinoa	5 tbs
Hamish Bits	3 ½ tbs
Sweet Peas	1 ½ tbs
Carrots	1 tbs
Chicken Bouillon or Powder	1 tsp

Quinoa	4 tbs
Jerky	2 oz
Green Beans	3 tbs
Butternut Squash	3 tbs
Beef Bouillon or Powder	1 tsp

....

Quinoa	4 tbs
Jerky	2 oz
Green Beans	3 tbs
Butternut Squash	3 tbs
Beef Bouillon or Powder	1 tsp

....

Quinoa	7 ½ tbs
Jerky	2 oz
Broccoli	2 ½ tbs
Beef Bouillon or Powder	1 tsp

....

Quinoa	6 tbs
Jerky	2 oz
Green Beans	1 ½ tbs
Butternut Squash	1 ½ tbs
Beef Bouillon or Powder	1 tsp

Quinoa	7 tbs
Jerky	2 oz
Sweet Peas	1 tbs
Carrots	1 tbs
Beef Bouillon or Powder	1 tsp

. . . .

Quinoa	7 tbs
Jerky	2 oz
Carrots	1 tbs
Celery	1 tbs
Beef Bouillon or Powder	1 tsp

. . . .

Quinoa	7 tbs
Jerky	2 oz
Peppers, mixed	1 ½ tbs
Corn	2 tbs
Beef Bouillon or Powder	1 tsp

RICE

Rice	4 tbs
Beefish Bits	4 tbs
Carrots	2 tsp
Celery	2 tsp
Beef Bouillon or Powder	1 tsp

Rice	4 tbs
Beefish Bits	3 tbs
Peppers, mixed	2 tbs
Corn	2 tbs
Beef Bouillon or Powder	1 tsp

Rice	5 tbs
Beefish Bits	3 ½ tbs
Broccoli	3 tbs
Beef Bouillon or Powder	1 tsp

Rice	5 tbs
Beefish Bits	3 tbs
Sweet Peas	1 ½ tbs
Carrots	1 ½ tbs
Beef Bouillon or Powder	1 tsp

Rice	4 tbs
Beefish Bits	3 tbs
Green Beans	1 ½ tbs
Butternut Squash	1 ½ tbs
Beef Bouillon or Powder	1 tsp

. . . .

Rice	4 tbs
Chickenish Bits	4 tbs
Carrots	1 ½ tbs
Celery	1 ½ tbs
Chicken Bouillon or Powder	1 tsp

. . . .

Rice	5 tbs
Chickenish Bits	4 tbs
Peppers, mixed	1 tbs
Corn	1 tbs
Chicken Bouillon or Powder	1 tsp

. . . .

Rice	4 tbs
Chickenish bits	4 tbs
Sweet Peas	1 ½ tbs
Carrots	1 ½ tbs
Chicken Bouillon or Powder	1 tsp

Rice	5 ½ tbs
Chickenish bits	4 tbs
Broccoli	2 tbs
Chicken Bouillon or Powder	1 tsp

. . . .

Rice	5 tbs
Chickenish Bits	3 tbs
Green Beans	1 ½ tbs
Butternut Squash	1 tbs
Chicken Bouillon or Powder	1 tsp

. . . .

Rice	5 tbs
Hamish Bits	4 tbs
Carrots	1 tbs
Celery	1 tbs
Chicken Bouillon or Powder	1 tsp

. . . .

Rice	5 tbs
Hamish Bits	4 tbs
Peppers, mixed	1 ½ tbs
Corn	1 ½ tbs
Chicken Bouillon or Powder	1 tsp

Rice	4 ½ tbs
Hamish Bits	5 tbs
Sweet Peas	2 tbs
Chicken Bouillon or Powder	1 tsp

....

Rice	4 tbs
Hamish Bits	4 tbs
Green Beans	1 ½ tbs
Butternut Squash	1 ½ tbs
Chicken Bouillon or Powder	1 tsp

....

Rice	5 ½ tbs
Hamish Bits	4 tbs
Broccoli	3 tbs
Chicken Bouillon or Powder	1 tsp

....

Rice	6 tbs
Hamish Bits	3 ½ tbs
Sweet Peas	1 ½ tbs
Carrots	1 tbs
Chicken Bouillon or Powder	1 tsp

Rice	6 tbs
Jerky	2 oz
Green Beans	2 ½ tbs
Butternut Squash	2 tbs
Beef Bouillon or Powder	1 tsp

....

Rice	6 tbs
Jerky	2 oz
Green Beans	2 tbs
Butternut Squash	2 ½ tbs
Beef Bouillon or Powder	1 tsp

....

Rice	8 ½ tbs
Jerky	2 oz
Broccoli	3 tbs
Beef Bouillon or Powder	1 tsp

....

Rice	7 tbs
Jerky	2 oz
Green Beans	1 ½ tbs
Butternut Squash	1 ½ tbs
Beef Bouillon or Powder	1 tsp

Rice	7 ½ tbs
Jerky	2 oz
Sweet Peas	1 ½ tbs
Carrots	1 tbs
Beef Bouillon or Powder	1 tsp

....

Rice	7 tbs
Jerky	2 oz
Carrots	1 ½ tbs
Celery	1 ½ tbs
Beef Bouillon or Powder	1 tsp

....

Rice	7 tbs
Jerky	2 oz
Peppers, mixed	2 ½ tbs
Corn	2 tbs
Beef Bouillon or Powder	1 tsp

WILD RICE

Wild Rice	6 ½ tbs
Beefish Bits	4 tbs
Carrots	2 tsp
Celery	2 tsp
Beef Bouillon or Powder	1 tsp

Wild Rice	3 tbs
Beefish Bits	3 tbs
Peppers, mixed	1 tbs
Corn	1 tbs
Beef Bouillon or Powder	1 tsp

Wild Rice	3 ½ tbs
Beefish Bits	3 tbs
Broccoli	3 tsp
Beef Bouillon or Powder	1 tsp

Wild Rice	3 tbs
Beefish Bits	2 ½ tbs
Sweet Peas	1 tbs
Carrots	1 tbs
Beef Bouillon or Powder	1 tsp

Wild Rice	3 tbs
Beefish Bits	2 ½ tbs
Green Beans	1 tbs
Butternut Squash	1 tbs
Beef Bouillon or Powder	1 tsp

. . . .

Wild Rice	3 tbs
Chickenish Bits	2 tbs
Carrots	2 tbs
Celery	2 tbs
Chicken Bouillon or Powder	1 tsp

. . . .

Wild Rice	3 ½ tbs
Chickenish Bits	3 tbs
Peppers, mixed	1 tbs
Corn	1 tbs
Chicken Bouillon or Powder	1 tsp

. . . .

Wild Rice	3 tbs
Chickenish bits	3 tbs
Sweet Peas	1 ½ tbs
Carrots	1 ½ tbs
Chicken Bouillon or Powder	1 tsp

Wild Rice	3 ½ tbs
Chickenish bits	3 tbs
Broccoli	3 tbs
Chicken Bouillon or Powder	1 tsp

. . . .

Wild Rice	3 tbs
Chickenish bits	3 tbs
Green Beans	1 ½ tbs
Butternut Squash	1 tbs
Chicken Bouillon or Powder	1 tsp

. . . .

Wild Rice	3 tbs
Hamish Bits	3 tbs
Carrots	1 ½ tbs
Celery	1 tbs
Chicken Bouillon or Powder	1 tsp

. . . .

Wild Rice	3 ½ tbs
Hamish Bits	3 tbs
Peppers, mixed	1 tbs
Corn	1 tbs
Chicken Bouillon or Powder	1 tsp

Wild Rice	3 tbs
Hamish Bits	4 tbs
Sweet Peas	2 tbs
Chicken Bouillon or Powder	1 tsp

. . . .

Wild Rice	3 tbs
Hamish Bits	2 ½ tbs
Green Beans	1 ½ tbs
Butternut Squash	1 ½ tbs
Chicken Bouillon or Powder	1 tsp

. . . .

Wild Rice	3 ½ tbs
Hamish Bits	4 tbs
Broccoli	2 ½ tbs
Beef Bouillon or Powder	1 tsp

. . . .

Wild Rice	3 tbs
Hamish Bits	3 ½ tbs
Sweet Peas	1 ½ tbs
Carrots	1 tbs
Chicken Bouillon or Powder	1 tsp

Wild Rice	3 tbs
Jerky	2 oz
Green Beans	3 tbs
Butternut Squash	2 ½ tbs
Beef Bouillon or Powder	1 tsp

. . . .

Wild Rice	3 tbs
Jerky	2 oz
Green Beans	3 tbs
Butternut Squash	2 ½ tbs
Beef Bouillon or Powder	1 tsp

. . . .

Wild Rice	5 tbs
Jerky	2 oz
Broccoli	2 ½ tbs
Beef Bouillon or Powder	1 tsp

. . . .

Wild Rice	4 tbs
Jerky	2 oz
Green Beans	1 ½ tbs
Butternut Squash	1 ½ tbs
Beef Bouillon or Powder	1 tsp

Wild Rice	4 ½ tbs
Jerky	2 oz
Sweet Peas	1 ½ tbs
Carrots	1 tbs
Beef Bouillon or Powder	1 tsp

. . . .

Wild Rice	4 ½ tbs
Jerky	2 oz
Carrots	1 tbs
Celery	1 tbs
Beef Bouillon or Powder	1 tsp

. . . .

Wild Rice	4 ½ tbs
Jerky	2 oz
Peppers, mixed	1 ½ tbs
Corn	2 tbs
Beef Bouillon or Powder	1 tsp

OATMEAL

To make a container of oatmeal that uses one cup of water, use 10 tbs of oatmeal; for a somewhat thinner consistency, use 9 tsp of oatmeal.

Oatmeal	10 tbs
Brown Sugar	4 tsp
Cinnamon	¾ tsp

. . . .

Oatmeal	10 tbs
Dried Apples	3 tbs
Cinnamon	¾ tsp
Sliced Almonds	2 tbs (optional)

. . . .

Oatmeal	10 tbs
Dried Berries	2 tbs
Pecan Pieces	2 tbs

Note: Nutmeg, Allspice, Clove, Pumpkin Pie Spice, or other spices can all be substituted for the cinnamon without a problem. Even cocoa could be added to the mixture.

Note: Any nut, including pine nuts, can be substituted for the pecan pieces or almonds, as preferred.

Note: Most dried fruits will work well, here. Freeze-dried fruits, however, may well crush when vacuum sealed, but they will still add flavor. Moist, dried fruits—figs, dates, some kinds of dried apricots, etc—will not store well at room temperature for long, and probably should be avoided.

Note: Other sugars, including maple sugar, can be used here as well.

JUST THE GRAINS

In scenarios where it is appropriate to plan to trap game for adding to the pot, it may be useful to have dried grain pouches planned to be added to water to prepare as a side for the game, or to cook with the game. Here are the amounts of each grain to vacuum seal to add to one cup (240 ml) of water.

Amaranth	5 tbs + 1 tsp
Barley	6 tbs + 1 tsp
Buckwheat	8 tbs
Bulgur	8 tbs
Cracked Wheat	5 tbs + 1 tsp
Lentils	5 tbs + 1 tsp
Quinoa	8 tbs
Rice	9 tbs + 1 tsp
Wild Rice	5 tbs + 1 tsp

Note: all measures are approximate; grains may vary slightly in the amount of water absorbed.

CREDITS

This volume was created with advice and assistance from the Department of Nutritional Science at the University of Illinois, Urbana-Champaign, Illinois. All errata are the author's and should not be taken to reflect on that department.

The staff of the University of Illinois College of Medicine Library, Peoria Campus, have also been of immense assistance in creating this short work.

My beloved wife Carol deserves credit for her amazing patience, as I have squandered hours of time that I could have spent with her, tending to her needs and desires, in producing this text.

All credit and glory that may accrue from this work goes to my Lord and Savior, Jesus Christ; all that is wrong, I attribute to my own fallen state.

NOTES:

NOTES:

NOTES:

NOTES:

Made in the USA
Las Vegas, NV
16 September 2023

77694214R00046